Pierre the Penguin

the

A True Story

Written by **Jean Marzollo** and illustrated by **Laura Regan**

SCHOLASTIC INC. New York Toronto London Auckland Sydney Mexico City New Delhi Hong Kong

This book is dedicated to Pierre the Penguin, Senior Aquatic Biologist Pam Schaller, and all the other people at San Francisco's California Academy of Sciences—an aquarium, planetarium, and natural history museum all under one roof. The people there love our world. They study it and share with others what they learn. They are very happy to share with you in this book what they have learned about penguins.

For the kids and teachers at Haldane Elementary School and the Philipstown Recreation Learning Center, my thanks for your helpful feedback. For Irene O'Garden, my thanks for your poetic advice. For Aimee Jackson at Sleeping Bear Press, thanks for all of your help and encouragement.

J. M.

For Peter, my own Pierre, with love!

L. R.

ISBN 978-0-545-34640-5

Text copyright © 2010 by Jean Marzollo.
Illustration copyright © 2010 by Laura Regan. All rights reserved. Published by Scholastic Inc., 557 Broadway, New York, NY 10012, by arrangement with Sleeping Bear Press™. SCHOLASTIC and associated logos are trademarks and/or registered trademarks of Scholastic Inc.

12 11 10 9 8 7 6 5 4 3 2 1   11 12 13 14 15 16/0

Printed in the U.S.A.   40

This edition first printing, October 2011

Downloadable teachers' guides available:
http://www.gale.cengage.com/pdf/TeachersGuides/PenguinGuide.pdf

This is the true story of Pierre, a small penguin in a big museum. It is also about the people at the California Academy of Sciences who worked together to help him through a hard time.

Down at the end of African Hall,
past statues of animals **big** and **small**,

there's an aquarium **wide** and **tall**,
with real live **penguins**, 20 in all!

African penguins don't like ice.
For them, a warmer place is nice.

Here comes **Pam** with **fish** in her **pail**.
The penguins are fed twice a day without **fail**.

Pam enters the tank through the sky-painted **wall**.
A hidden door there leads out to a **hall**.

Some of the penguins look just the **same**.
Wing bands help Pam call the **birds** by name.

One day aquatic biologist Pam,
observing the penguins, saw one in a jam.

Gently, gently, she examined Pierre.
His feathers were gone.
His bottom was bare.

Pierre was afraid to go for a swim.
He'd get too cold if he dived right in.

"How can I help you? What can I do?"
Pam had ideas and tried the first two.

She tried a heater, and the vet prescribed pills.
But nothing worked.
Pierre shivered still.

The other penguins grew afraid of Pierre.
He looked so strange that he gave them a **scare**.

They **brayed** at him as he **shivered** on **shore**.
They made him feel worse than he felt **before**.

One rainy day biologist Pam
came up with a new idea—Shazam!

"My dog wears a raincoat," she told the vet.
"Could Pierre wear a wetsuit?" The vet said,
"You bet!"

Pam and a friend worked day and night
to make a pattern that fit just **right**.

Then a wetsuit was made of **neoprene**—
the tiniest one you've ever **seen**.

Carefully, Pam put on **Pierre** a wetsuit a **featherless** penguin could **wear.**

Standing on a rock in his new wetsuit,
Pierre the Penguin looked mighty cute.

He felt nice and warm, and he wanted to swim. So what did he do? He dived right in.

Now **Pierre** stood **proud** and **tall**,
and nobody brayed at him at **all**.

Six weeks went by, and then a **surprise** . . .
Pam could hardly believe her **eyes**.

Not only was **Pierre** no longer **cold**.
He had **NEW** feathers! Observe and **behold**.

Now warm in water, now warm on shore,
guess who didn't need his wetsuit anymore!

Pierre made a nest for his very best friend.
Their story goes on, thanks to Pam.

The End.

Questions from Kids with Answers from Pam

Pam Schaller, Senior Aquatic Biologist, California Academy of Sciences

Why is the hall called African Hall?
Because it has African animals in it.

Why did Pierre lose his feathers?
African penguins "molt" or replace their feathers every year. Pierre skipped molting for a few years so his feathers became brittle and broke off.

Why did they grow back?
The wetsuit kept Pierre warm enough so that he could put his energy into growing new feathers.

How old was Pierre when he lost his feathers?
He was about 24 years old. Pierre hatched from his egg on February 16, 1983.

Why does your dog have a raincoat?
My dog came from warm Hawaii. Her raincoat helps her stay warm and dry in cool Northern California rain.

What is a "wetsuit"?
A tight-fitting rubber suit that helps people stay warm in the water. I wear a wetsuit when I go into the penguin tank.

Why did Pierre need a wetsuit?
To keep him warm and help him float while he swam.

What is "neoprene"?
A soft rubbery fabric used to make most wetsuits.

Why are the penguins' wing bands different colors?
The colors are different for each penguin when they are young. When they get older, they form pairs, and I change the color of their bands. Penguin couples have matching-colored wing bands.

Why are the wing bands on different wings?
Males have bands on their right wings. Females have bands on their left wings.

What is an "aquatic biologist"?
Biologists study living things. Aquatic means water. (Hence, "aquarium.") An aquatic biologist studies animals that live in water.

What other kinds of scientists are there?
We have scientists who study all types of life including botanists, who study plants, and entomologists, who study insects.

What does "bray" mean?
It's the sound that donkeys make. African penguins bray when they are protecting their territory. Penguins also bray to identify each other.

What does "shazam" mean?
It's an expression people say when something surprises them.

Does the hidden door lead out to African Hall?
No, it leads out to another hall that leads to my office.

The wall and ceiling are painted like the sky. Are the rocks real?
The rocks are made by people to look like rocks found in Boulders Beach, South Africa. That's one of the places African penguins live in the wild.

Are penguins really birds?
Yes. Birds are covered with feathers, have wings, and lay eggs. Penguins use their wings to swim. Sometimes their wings are called flippers.

Can penguins fly?
No. Penguins' wings are not long enough to lift them up in the air.

Can penguins eat while swimming?
Yes! In the wild, African penguins catch and eat fish while in the ocean.

Can penguins breathe under water?
No, penguins have lungs (like people) so they must hold their breath while they swim under water.

How many kinds of penguins are there?
There are 17 species or different kinds of penguins.

Do other aquatic biologists know about Pierre?
Yes. I shared Pierre's wetsuit pattern with other biologists. It is important to share information so we can learn from each other.

Is it true that we can see the penguins online?
Yes! Just go to www.calacademy.org/webcams/penguins. You'll be able to see what our penguins are doing right now! You might even see me or another biologist feed them!